GIRAFFE GIRL

LAUREN WADSWORTH

PublishAmerica
Baltimore

First printing

ISBN: 1-4137-8613-8
PUBLISHED BY PUBLISHAMERICA, LLLP
www.publishamerica.com
Baltimore

Printed in the United States of America

I would like to dedicate this book to my mom, my angel. Her love and motivation has given me the inner strength to keep going every day and to believe that I can achieve anything I put my mind to.

Acknowledgments

I would like to thank my family for all their love and support throughout the years. My mom, for listening to all my problems and keeping my secrets. My dad, for giving up everything to ensure that I was happy. My sister Amber, for all the sisterly love and for providing a shoulder for me to cry on. My brother Bud, for cracking me up when I was down, and Dave, for being there for me when I needed a hug. I would like to thank my best friend, Kristy, for making me laugh and keeping my spirits up. To my good friend Holly, I cherish you. Thank you for understanding. I would like to say thanks to my team in the fight to live. Dr. Joel Oger, thank you for saving my life. Thank you to my dear Grandma Pat for all the love and prayers; they truly made all the difference. Thank you to my Grandpa Bauder for being there when I needed you. To Bob Price, for inspiring me to get back up no matter how many times I get knocked down. To Maya, for all your sweet suggestions and hilarious comments. My uncle Greg, for all the encouragement and tips. To all the people who prayed for me in my time of need, thank you. Thank you to the rest of the people who influenced my life.

CHAPTER 1-
LIVING THE GOOD LIFE

As a little girl, I was an outgoing, charismatic, spontaneous wild child. I was, and still am, extremely stubborn, with a zest for life. I loved rollerblading, riding my bike, swimming, animals, dancing, and sports of all kinds. I performed in an array of dance classes, from ballet to jazz. I also participated in sports of all types, excelling in baseball. In the summer of 1994, I took the gold medal for our team for the second year in a row. I was awarded the titles of "farthest thrower" and "Most Valuable Player" in my league.

I was a star student and was well liked by my peers as well as by the older kids in higher grades. I got a thrill from shocking people with my unpredictable behavior. As a youngster, I was a happy child but, like most, difficult at times.

Almost every day my parents would say, "Lauren, Don't leave the block!" as firmly as possible to let me know they meant business, but, within seconds, I'd be off on my bike until sunset, when they'd hunt me down. Getting me inside to eat or take a bath was nearly impossible. I was like a filthy little pig, squealing and squirming as they chucked me into the tub and hosed me down. My charm was sweet, but my curiosity often got the best of me.

This is a picture of me when I was two years old. As you can see, I loved to make people laugh and often did random things to get people's attention.

This is my sister, Amber, and me at Disneyland.

When I was three years old, my parents took me to Disneyland. There was a group of older Spanish men playing salsa music. I jumped into the center of the crowd surrounding them and started dancing provocatively. As I danced, I was driven by the crowd's cheers and whistles. I just had to be the center of attention.

When I was five years old, I was picked out of all the children in my kindergarten class to appear on the front page of the local newspaper. The article was showcasing children that would spend extra time in kindergarten because of their birth date, and I was one of them. Realizing that, for them to pick me, I had to be cute only made my ego bigger, and, when they asked me to put on a "pouty face," I did it with ease because I just used the face I normally did to get my way. Whenever anyone would get mad at me, I'd say, "Have you seen my hair lately?" in my sweetest, most charming voice as I played with my perfectly shaped, waist-length blonde ringlets.

Then there was the time when I was six and I decided to put our cat, Cassie, in the microwave to "see what would happen." Luckily, I didn't know how to start the microwave, and, after I asked my dad to start it for me, he found her and rescued her.

I lived at home with my parents and two siblings, a brother we nicknamed "Bud" and a sister, Amber. My mother, Karen, was an assertive, aggressive, talkative woman with piercing hazel eyes and a strong will. She grew up in the east end of Vancouver and had a rough life, filled with tragedy. My dad, Mike, was a humble, warm-hearted, down-to-earth brainiac who grew up in a southern, structured, strict, loving family. My sister, Amber, was a loud, domineering mother-figure who was five years older than me. My baby brother, Bud, was a hilarious, sensitive practical joker who was three years younger than me. We weren't a rich family, but both my parents worked, and we had enough to get by. A typical day in my life would be getting up for school and either getting a ride with my sister or walking with my good friend, Ashley, who lived a block away. After school, I'd either attend soccer, baseball, or dance practice. On a hectic day, I sometimes attended more than one. My mom was home during the day and would take my brother to kindergarten, while my dad worked. My dad usually picked us up after school on his way home from work. We'd get home and see mom briefly before she headed off to work until midnight.

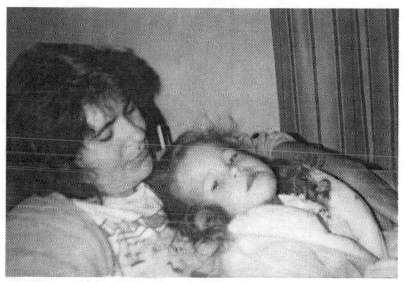

This is one of my favorite pictures of my mom and me .

Most weekends, when I wasn't busy, were spent at my best friend Kristy's house. She lived in another city about 40 minutes away. Our moms had been best friends since they were twelve, and we were carrying on the tradition. Kristy was exactly like me, and we fit perfectly, like lock and key, but together either we found trouble or trouble found us. One morning, we got Frosted Wheats in the mail as a sample. We went around the entire neighborhood, ransacking mailboxes for their cereal samples. Kristy had four brothers and sisters; I was also friends with her two sisters, Holly and Sasha. One night, the four of us decided to sneak out the bedroom window and play Nicky Nicky Nine Door on the neighbors, who were constantly annoyed by us. Our usual routine consisted of walking to the nearby 7-11 to steal candy before heading to the local school to sit atop the roof. We were great friends, and I could always depend on Kristy for anything. Everything was going great. I had a great family with a good, structured home life. I had tons of friends and interests. For the most part, we were just a typical family, living a normal life, and then everything changed.

CHAPTER 2– SOMETHING'S AWRY

It was a windy, crisp day in October, and, like I usually did on days when I had dance, I came home from school and got ready. It was a special day because that evening was my ballet dance recital. My mom had taken off work, and I was ecstatic that both my parents would be there, equipped with a camera. I was an amazing ballerina, and, as I performed, I could see my parents smiling, proud as they watched.

Three-quarters through the performance, I suddenly felt shaky and tired. As I turned to spin in my soft pink tutu, my legs suddenly gave out from under me. I sat in a heap on the ground for a few seconds, puzzled as to why I was unable to get up. After helping me to the side of the gymnasium, my parents hugged me as I watched, through tear-filled eyes, the rest of the girls finish the recital without me.

The next day, my dad took me to see the family doctor. He said that it was probably just a pulled muscle and that we shouldn't worry. We didn't think much of it until three weeks later when a similar event occurred.

This is me on the night of my ballet recital, just minutes before I collapsed.

It was a Saturday in November, and my dad was off work that day. He was taking me to the movies to see a movie that I'd been dying to see. I was overexcited that day, singing and carrying on during the whole drive to the theater. When we got there, the movie was packed, and, after standing in line for an hour, they announced that the movie was sold out. Realizing that I wasn't going to get to see the movie, I headed back to the car with my head hanging low. Irritated and disappointed, I started crying until, seconds later, I collapsed. As my dad looked at me sitting on the ground, he had a look of puzzlement on his face, wondering why I was still sitting there. I attempted to get up, but, after numerous tries, I started to cry about the lack of cooperation from my body.

"Lauren, get up now!"

"No, I can't!" My voice was muffled by tears.

He started to get angry and thought I was throwing a temper tantrum. He pulled me up by my arm, and I stood up shakily. The whole way home, I stared out the dirty, stained window, wondering what had happened and wishing that my dad wasn't mad at me.

A week later, I was coming out of class. It was sunny and warm outside, and a perfect day to walk. I went outside, searching for my sister, with whom I was to walk, when suddenly I got a strange feeling. It was the same feeling I had gotten before, at the dance recital. Not exactly sure what this feeling was, I told my sister that I couldn't walk home.

"Lauren, why can't you walk home?" my sister asked, intrigued

"I don't know. I just can't; it's too far," I said.

She immediately thought that I was being stubborn and didn't want to walk that day. After arguing with me for a few minutes, she gave up and called a cab. I sat in a chair in the office with her while we waited for a cab. A few minutes later, a pale, white, four-door cab pulled up. I walked across the parking lot to the cab and fell, face first, to the ground. I started crying as I once again found myself on the ground, unable to move my legs. My sister, already irritated, began yelling at me to get up.

"I can't; I can't!" I pleaded, as she picked me up and threw me in the cab, face first against the seat. I lay there, unable to move as I panted and cried. My breathing felt shallow, and I was confused by what was happening to me. We arrived at my house, and my dad came out to pay the cab driver. My dad helped me out of the car and into the house.

A few days later, my mom asked me to go downstairs and get the mail for her. Preoccupied with other things, I made a fuss and then finally went. I had retrieved the mail and had begun to climb the second flight of stairs when I got a strange feeling of weakness. I fell in the middle of the stairs and called out to my mom. My mom came running, and I told her that I couldn't move my legs. She began yelling at me and said, "Lauren, if you want attention, there are other ways to go about getting it."

As she turned and left me to sit all alone on the stairs, helplessly, I couldn't help but cry in confusion. After I sat there for a few minutes, the feeling of weakness passed, and I returned to normal, able to climb up the rest of the stairs.

At school, a pair of twin boys had been physically abusing me, so the combination of that and my recent behavior made my parents decide to send me to the school counselor. The counselor would ask me various questions and do activities with me, but he and my parents were both convinced that I was faking these episodes for attention.

✳✳✳

About a month passed. It was a misty January evening, and I was taking my nightly bath. As usual, my parents had a hard time getting me in the tub, but, after finally agreeing, I jumped in and began splashing around.

I had dipped my head back to wash the soap out of my hair when that "feeling" suddenly came over me. As I quickly realized I couldn't sit back up, I panicked and cried out for my parents. Unable to lift my head out of the water, I was inhaling water. My parents came in and sat me up as I flailed my arms out to them for help.

"Okay, get out of the tub," my mom said to me, and, after hearing

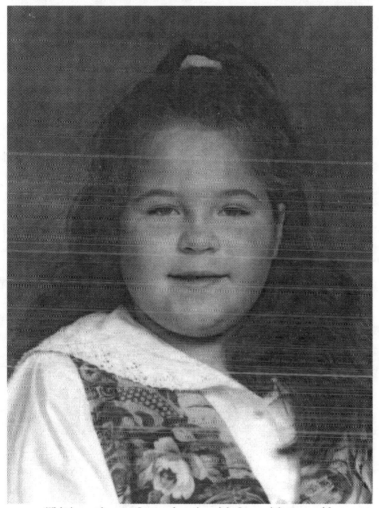

This is me the year I started getting sick. I was eight years old.
My eyes drooped, and my smile was a funny sneer.

the phrase "I can't" again, my mom got angry and pulled me up out of the tub onto the ledge. I stumbled over, falling to the ground. I started crying, which only angered my mom and dad even more. She spanked my bottom but, after I made a gurgling noise and remained still, a look of worry crossed her face.

My dad started yelling at me. "You listen to your mother!" he screamed. As I lay there, unresponsive, confused, and crying, he slapped my face and continued to yell. My mom stopped him.

"No, Mike, there's something wrong; this isn't normal. We need a doctor!" she hollered.

"Sometimes we have to be doctors!" he shouted back.

"No, Mike! Please! There's something wrong; we need to take her to the hospital!" my mom begged. As I sat on the cold bathroom floor, trembling, my mom returned to help me up. She got me into my room and into bed. As I lay with her next to me, with a muffled voice, I said, "I'm sorry, mom."

"It's okay, honey," she said in her endearing voice as she rubbed my forehead. A couple of days later, my dad took me back to see the family doctor, explaining to him the events that had taken place. He didn't know what to make of it, so he sent me to see a pediatrician.

At school, I could no longer go outside at lunch or recess to play with the other kids. My teacher told my parents that, in gym, I shuffled my feet and breathed heavily.

✳ ✳ ✳

A couple of days passed, and it was time for me to see the pediatrician. They brought me into an examination room that had bright colors and Disney stickers all over the walls. It helped to ease my nervousness while I waited for the doctor to come in. The door flew open, and in came a middle aged, flamboyant, white-haired man.

"You must be Lauren!" he exclaimed. "I'm Dr. Brown," he said as he held out his hand to greet me.

"Nice to meet you!" I beamed back.

He asked me to perform various tasks and tested me physically on both sides, noting that the left side was much different than the right. He told my dad he thought that I might have a brain tumor and that I'd need some additional testing. For the next couple of weeks, I sat, every day, in the old brown- and orange-flowered chair, watching *Saved By The Bell* reruns. I could no longer go to school because I couldn't walk or hardly even move. I couldn't smile or clamp my teeth together to chew. Swallowing and breathing was difficult, and my eyes drooped like a St. Bernard's.

I just sat there, all day, with dark circles around my eyes, looking like a stroke victim. Any time I had to go somewhere, my dad carried me. My parents fed me soups and juices to maintain my nutrition. Normally a chubby little girl, I had now lost about fifteen pounds. The doctor was still awaiting test results from the EKG and CAT scan, and, as the days passed, I was slowly dying.

Until one night...

CHAPTER 3- CRISIS

I had developed an ear infection, so Dad took me to the clinic. At this point, I was upset and felt like I was paralyzed, and I had a thick saliva in my mouth. The doctor didn't acknowledge these symptoms but diagnosed me with an ear infection. He prescribed me penicillin and sent me on my way.

My dad took me home, carried me up the two long flights of stairs, and put me into bed. The next morning, I awoke even worse than the day before. I was still in a state of stupor, unable to move, swallow, or chew, barely able talk and breathe. My dad was worried and was thinking of taking me to the hospital when, around seven p.m., Dr. Brown gave us a ring.

"Hello?" my dad said nervously.

"This is Dr. Brown calling; can I speak to Mr. Wadsworth please?"

"Oh, yes, this is Michael Wadsworth. I'm glad you called."

"Well, I wanted to let you know Lauren's test results from the EKG and CAT scan came back completely normal. How is she doing?"

"She's not doing well. She's completely unable to walk or eat…uhhhh…" He stammered in his thick Texas accent before continuing. "She's having trouble breathing, she can hardly hold her head up or her eyes open, and there is a thick saliva coming from her mouth. I took her to the clinic last night, and they said that she has an ear infection and gave her penicillin. Look, I'm getting really worried. She's been in this state for two days now, and it's getting worse."

"Hmmm. I have an idea as to what it may be. I'm on call here tonight in the ER, so I think you should bring her on down," he advised.

"All right, see you in a little bit. Bye-bye."

He hung up the phone and walked into my room to break the news to me. "Lauren, I need to take you to the hospital."

Those nine words made my gut turn and struck me like a whip inflicting pain. In a heartbeat, I began to go into crisis mode. My tears flowed like a river, drowning me in terror. My hysteria only seemed to worsen the situation because the saliva was now so thick and glue-like that you could string it out three feet. My breathing was pursy, and I struggled for air.

My dad got me some water, but that only worsened the situation when I began choking on it, unable to swallow. My brother was watching the horrible scene. Scared and confused, he picked up the phone and dialed my mom's work number. "Mommy, come home please," he begged as he cried into the telephone.

Neither my dad nor my brother had ever seen me this bad, and my dad panicked as he tried to clear my throat. My dad grabbed the phone from my petrified brother and told my mom that we were going to the hospital. I was still choking and frantic as my dad picked me up over his shoulder and carried me down the stairs and put me into the car. He climbed in and looked in the glove compartment for napkins. He wiped the scum, which was now completely blocking my airway, from my mouth. I laid my head against the headrest; dazed and struggling to breathe, I heaved hard and gurgled.

My dad pulled over two more times to clear my mouth, an effort which was making little difference as I was now turning blue. My dad pulled up at the emergency entrance and ran inside, yelling, "I need help! I need help!" Within seconds, a nurse and my dad ran back out with a wheelchair. They got me into the wheelchair, and, as my head fell back lifelessly, the nurse slapped my face lightly and yelled at me to hang in there. She quickly pushed me through the glass sliding doors and into the back.

As they got me onto a stretcher bed, I searched like a private detective for a breath of air. They stuck a tube into my throat to suction the built-up saliva and gave me oxygen. I felt a rush of air into my lungs. Finally. Air. I could breathe. Dr. Brown came to my bedside and examined me. He then prepared to do a "tensilon test."

The tensilon test was a method of diagnosing the disease myasthenia gravis, a chronic autoimmune neuromuscular disease characterized by varying degrees of weakness of the skeletal voluntary muscles of the body. The nature of myasthenia gravis is muscle weakness that increases during periods of activity and improves after periods of rest. Myasthenia gravis is caused by a defect in the transmission of nerve impulses to muscles. Normally, when impulses travel down the nerve, the nerve endings release a neurotransmitter substance called acetylcholine. In the case of myasthenia gravis, antibodies produced by the body's own immune system block, alter, or destroy the receptors for acetylcholine. Tensilon inhibits acetylcholinesterase and prolongs the presence of the neurotransmitter, acetylcholine, in the neuromuscular junction, resulting in enhanced muscle strength.

The doctor had three needles, one with tensilon and the other two with an antidote in case the diagnosis was wrong, and my heart stopped. As I lay there, nervous and tired, he administered the tensilon, and, within seconds, I coughed for the first time in months. I was able to speak clearly and move around. The tensilon only lasted a few minutes, and then I returned to my sluggish ways. Dr. Brown told my dad that they'd have to keep me overnight.

Later that night, my dad called my mom at home to tell her what had happened. My dad handed me the phone, and I told my mom happily that my problem was solved. I'll never forget her words: "Great, you'll be back to school Monday!" Boy, was she wrong.

CHAPTER 4 – THE FIRST STEPS OF A LONG JOURNEY

The next morning, I awoke feeling much better. A nurse had stayed by my bedside during the night. I was feeling happier now that I was getting better; I even ate breakfast that morning for the first time in a month. I called Kristy and told her that I was in the hospital. She said she'd come visit me when her mom had a day off work.

That afternoon, Dr. Brown came to see me. Unknown to me, he had told my parents that I'd need to be transferred to a hospital specifically for children where I'd have a thymectomy, a procedure that involves the cutting of the ribs and removal of the thymus, located behind the heart. The thymus, a gland in the body that produces antibodies, is removed in patients diagnosed with myasthenia gravis to aid in stopping the production of antibodies. Dr. Brown told me that I'd be transferred to another hospital. I was confused because I thought that I was better and could go home.

I was transferred by ambulance that afternoon to the new hospital, where I was met by my parents and siblings. They checked me in and took me to floor 3a, the neurology ward. This would be my home for the next month. They wheeled me into my new room, which I examined carefully. It had rainbow-colored pin-striped curtains and Disney characters sprawled across the walls, which didn't seem to ease my mind because I didn't want to be there. There was a medium-sized TV hanging in the center of the room above the four beds, each of which was situated in a corner. The occupants of the other beds were children, also, which I found intriguing.

Moments later, the nurse came in. She was a short, curly-haired woman with moss-green eyes.

"Hi! I'm Nancy! I'll be your nurse tonight until seven o'clock. You can get situated and put your belongings into this locker." She paused, pointing to the brown cupboard labeled "bed 1," then continued, "I'll need to get some information from your parents. Here's the call bell if you need anything; just ring it, and I'll come in."

My parents told me they'd be right back and left to go talk to the nurse. As I waited impatiently for them to come back, I looked over at the girl in the bed beside me. She had all kinds of tubes connected to her and had just come out of surgery. Little did I know that, in a couple of weeks, that would be me. I glanced around the rest of the room, intimidated by all the machines and sickness. As my parents came back into the room, I sighed a deep breath of relief and sat up on the edge of the bed.

"I'm ready to go now," I said mischievously.

My mom and dad pulled up the jungle-green, paneled metal chairs and sat down. "You can't go home yet; we have to get you better first," my dad replied.

"But I am better..." I trailed off in a muttered voice.

My dad slid up the rolling table in front of us and began to unwrap a deck of playing cards he had bought at the gift shop. "Lauren, look what I've got," he enticed me, holding up the deck of cards. My attention suddenly shifted from the little boy lying across from me to the slick new deck of cards that slid through his hands with ease as he shuffled. "Do you want to play?" he asked.

Still overwhelmed by my new surroundings, I nodded and steadily picked up the cards as he dealt them. "Crazy Eights," I mumbled. As we played, a group of men and woman in white coats suddenly burst into the room. We set our cards down and looked towards the crowd.

"Hi, I'm Dr. Falkland," one of the men said in a thick, rich Scottish accent. He had salt-and-pepper hair and looked to be in his mid-fifties. He was clearly the leader of the pack. "I'm a neurologist here, and I'll be overlooking your stay." He paused and then continued, "These are some of my colleagues, and they will be coming in to see you each day and doing some physical examinations with you."

He reached into his big black leather bag and pulled out a device that resembled a hammer. Wide-eyed, I watched as he tapped both my elbows and my knees. Then he asked me to push against him with my arms and legs, testing my strength. He told me to stare upwards for as long as I could and then to hold my breath and count as high as I could. He then turned to his colleagues and explained his findings in what sounded like a code. He said I would need to start on Mestinon, a drug used to treat myasthenia gravis.

Mestinon is a cholinesterase inhibitor that prevents the breakdown of acetylcholine by allowing more acetylcholine to accumulate. It would help improve my muscle weakness and symptoms. After starting the drug that day, I immediately felt tightness in my bowels and was extremely sweaty. I had to go to the bathroom frequently and felt intense stomach pain. However, it improved my symptoms within fifteen minutes each time I took it, and its effects generally lasted for four hours.

For the next three days, fifteen doctors would come in, one at a time, and repeat the same tests I had done with the Scottish doctor, each time exposing my disease and symptoms. I was told not to tell them what disease I had and was amused each time they guessed incorrectly. Only one out of all the doctors that came in guessed it right. "You're going to be a good doctor!" I exclaimed to him.

One time, they deliberately withheld my Mestinon so that I would be weaker. They then tested me while videotaping the procedure. They gave me tensilon again and taped me afterwards, showcasing the remarkable improvement. They made my parents sign waiver release forms that would allow them to use this video tape in universities to teach student doctors what to look for when diagnosing myasthenia gravis.

My parents had been staying with me every night since I arrived at the hospital and usually slept in the parents lounge or, if that was full, in the playroom on chairs. My thirteen-year-old sister stayed at home to look after my five-year-old brother, Bud, and take him to kindergarten on weekdays. My parents checked on them periodically and left them money for ordering food. Both my parents took off work to stay with me, and, when both of them couldn't be there, one or the other was with me.

After being in the hospital for about five days, I awoke to discover that the doctors were going to perform surgery on me to insert a line for plasmapheresis. This is a procedure that uses a big machine with a centrifuge that separates white blood cells from red blood cells. In my case, they discard the bad, antibody-filled plasma and replace it with albumin, which is filtered plasma from other people. This treatment would remove the buildup of antibodies from my blood and improve my symptoms.

I was going to undergo this treatment five times as a preparation for a thymectomy. I was still unaware at the time of the thymectomy for which I was being prepared. They just told me that having the plasmapheresis would make me feel better. Worried and scared, I began crying. The nurse came in with a cup of blue medicine and instructed me to drink it. After freaking out, I agreed to drink it and guzzled it down. It tasted so awful that I immediately got up and went into the bathroom to throw it up. The nurse got me back into the wheelchair and pushed me to the elevator with my parents.

"It'll be okay, Lauren, you'll be asleep," my mom said in her sweet, reassuring voice as the nurse pushed me out of the elevator and down a long hallway that had many signs and doors. I could feel my stomach turning with fear. A lady met us, and she had stuffed animals and electronic books with her to help distract me. She was extremely nice in attempting to calm me down, but it didn't work very well because I was hysterical.

They got me into a stretcher bed, and the nurse started an IV, which was a significant task to accomplish as it was. My parents saw that I was scared and frantic and tried to calm me. The doctor came in just then and explained that I'd be asleep and would feel nothing. I nervously agreed, and they administered some medication through the IV. My parents kissed me, and then I fell asleep.

The next morning, I awoke feeling groggy and nauseated. I immediately noticed the two port lines taped to the right side of my chest. A nurse came in and asked me if I wanted a blue popsicle, and I happily agreed.

A little while later, I was watching TV when I was interrupted by an older lady pushing a big machine. She told me that I was having plasmapheresis through my new line and that I'd feel a little tired afterwards but better in the days to follow. I was petrified but went forward with it, willing to do anything to get better so that I could go home. She connected a syringe to my line and began to flush it. As she did that, I started screaming, yelling, "STOP! It hurts! It hurts!"

The lady stopped and asked me where I felt pain. When I pointed to my line she thought for a moment and said, "Okay, Lauren, I just have to flush it once more to make sure of something. Be a brave girl, okay?"

I begged her not to and cried as she flushed it for the second time; again the same intense surge of pain shot through my chest, into my neck, and down my spine. "Okay, it's over, it's over," she assured me. She took her machine and left.

Half an hour later, the doctor came in, explaining that the line wasn't working and would need to be reinserted the following day. I was extremely upset, so my parents took me to the playroom, where I loved to go to play games and to make arts and crafts with the other kids. This helped to relax me and to keep my mind off the surgery. That night, I took forever to fall asleep, but both of my parents were there until I drifted off.

The next morning, the nurse came to get me, and, like before, I was irrational and crying. They put me to sleep and reinserted the line. I awoke the next day to find the lady with the big machine in the room again. She explained to me that this was a new, working line and that

27

things would go smoothly. I was petrified that I'd feel the same traumatic pain again, but, as she flushed the catheter, I felt nothing. The lady smiled. "See, it's not that bad."

I felt better about the situation and lay back in the bed. For the next two and half hours, my parents and I watched *Lady and The Tramp*, which Dr. Brown had taped for me. After the treatment was over, I was sleepy, so I took a little nap. My parents said that they had to go check on Amber and Bud but that they'd be back before I awoke.

I slept soundly through the night, and, the next morning when I awoke, I noticed that something was different. I felt stronger and could move about easier. Over the next week, I had plasmapheresis four more times, each time feeling better and better the next day. Excited and overjoyed, I ran up and down the stairs exclaiming to my parents, "Look! Look! I can go up stairs! I can walk! I'm better!"

Doctors started coming in groups again, each time testing my strength until I was worn out. Finally, my mom told them, "No more. She's tired." I thanked my mom and told her how happy I was to be better and to be going home soon. Little did I know that, on March 13th, my birthday, I was scheduled for my thymectomy.

My mom said, "Since your birthday's coming and you'll have to stay in the hospital a little bit longer, I was thinking that we could have a big party for you in the playroom and invite all your friends and family." Although I still wanted to go home, I agreed to the party at the hospital since I couldn't leave.

On the day of my party, I awoke early, excited by the coming day's events. From twelve noon until four in the afternoon, we'd be celebrating my birthday. All my friends, including Kristy and my family members, were there. We played games, opened presents, ate cake, sang, and cracked jokes while visiting with each other. It was a happy, fun-filled day, and it helped relieve the tension of the events that had happened.

Later that night, I was sitting on my bed, sorting through all my presents, while my parents watched television. Suddenly, there was a knock on the door. My dad got up and opened the door to a man in blue scrubs with a white mask dangling around his neck. My dad motioned for my mom to come over. She got up and went outside the door with my dad and the man, shutting the door behind them. I could hear them talking, but I couldn't hear exactly what was being said. All I heard was the word 'surgery.' Then it dawned on me, hitting me like a thousand bricks. They were being secretive, and the reason that I wasn't going home yet was that I was going to have surgery.

They came back in, and I immediately asked them if I was going to have surgery. They glanced at each other and then told me no, but I had a gut feeling that they were lying to me. The next morning, they came to take me, and I knew instantly that they had planned it all along. It was surgery again, but I couldn't understand why. I was doing so much better. As they took me down the hallway, I was once again met by the lady with toys and books to help calm and distract me, only this time I was even more hysterical. I felt betrayed by my own parents.

I stood up on the bed, screaming down the hallway to my parents, *"Don't let them do this to me! Don't let them cut me!"* I wanted to escape, and, as the doors shut with my parents behind it, crying, I felt completely alone.

After an unsuccessful hour of trying to calm me down, they called my parents back in. They gave me some medication through my IV to help me to settle down. The doctor explained to me as best he could why I had to have this surgery. I still didn't understand anything other than that I'd be better and playing baseball again in six months. My parents said that they'd be waiting for me when I came out and that everything would be fine.

Then they put me to sleep. The surgery went as planned, and I briefly awoke in the intensive care unit to see my parents and uncle Rodger, with whom I was close. It was three in the morning, and I was out of it because of the painkillers. I saw my parents and Rodger looking worriedly at me for about a minute, then I fell back into a deep sleep.

Over the next few days, I was slowly recovering. My chest was sore, but, with morphine, it wasn't too bad. Then came Sarah, a young nurse who decided to take me off the morphine and to give me Tylenol after I had just had my chest sawed open.

My mom had just fallen asleep, after days of no sleep at all, in the chair beside me when I awoke in terrible pain. My mom stayed up with me for hours while I cried in agony. After realizing that the nurse had taken the morphine drip away and had given me Tylenol instead, my mom lost her temper. She marched up to the nurses' station and asked for the head nurse. She told her that the doctor had said that I'd be on morphine for the first four days. She then told her to get out the log book.

"Whose signature is that?" She pointed to the signature on my order sheet.

"You don't understand, Mrs. Wadsworth. We all work together."

"*Whose signature is that?!*" my mom demanded, infuriated.

"It's mine," said Sarah.

"You've got a nurse who thinks she's a doctor," my mom said to the head nurse.

"Don't worry, Mrs. Wadsworth. We'll have a doctor up here as soon as possible. It's not a problem, really."

Within minutes, a doctor and my mom explained that the nurse had taken away the morphine and that I was in utter agony.

"I'm so sorry, Mrs. Wadsworth; there's been some sort of mix up. Get the morphine, Sarah," he said.

"But what about the—" Sarah started, but she was quickly cut off by the doctor.

"Sarah! The morphine! *Now!* I'm sorry, Mrs. Wadsworth. It's not a problem, really."

They got the morphine hooked up again, and, within minutes, I was pain-free and sleeping. Over the next few days, I slowly recovered, and my family and friends all came to see me. They put me into a chair each day for a couple of hours. My chest was sore but was healing. After being up and around for a whole day, the doctor came in and told me that I'd be going home the next day. I was thrilled.

On my final day at the hospital, I was seen again by the Scottish doctor. He told me that I'd be back to normal and playing baseball again in six months. I said goodbye to all the nurses and thanked them for everything. My parents collected my stuff, and we finally left. I was free.

CHAPTER 5- TRAPPED

As we got into the car and headed for home, I noticed that my dad was driving somewhere else.

"Where are we going?" I asked curiously.

"To our new house, a couple blocks from our old house. We had to move while you were in the hospital."

"Oh," I replied, wondering why they had failed to mention it.

We pulled up to a white house with red trim. It was directly across the street from my elementary school. I examined the outside of the house as my dad carefully helped me climb the huge cement stairs and then the next set inside. I looked around at the new, smaller house before heading down the hallway to my room, which I was to share with my little brother, Bud.

Angry and upset by the overwhelming new change, I put my head in my lap and began to cry. My dad came in the room and rubbed me on the back. "It'll be okay; don't worry, Doodle Bug." I wiped my eyes and began to put my stuff away.

Over the next couple of months, my disease steadily worsened instead of getting better like the doctors had predicted. My mom set up an appointment with the neurologist at the hospital, and, a few weeks later, I went to see her. We explained to her that my symptoms—double vision, difficulty walking, talking, chewing, swallowing—had returned.

The doctor told us that I'd have to start taking a medication called Prednisone. The medication would help to suppress my immune system, which, in turn, would suppress my disease. She explained that I would start on a high dosage for a few months and then taper off over a period of months. She also started me on Imuran, another immunosuppressive. I would need to get a blood test once a month to ensure the safety of my organs.

I went home and started taking the medication. Within weeks, I started to experience bad side effects. I began putting on weight and had severe insomnia and mood swings. Despite the medications, my myasthenia continued to worsen, and I was a very distraught nine-year-old. It was getting increasingly harder for me to walk even a short distance.

One day, I woke up and tried to walk down the hall to the bathroom, which was only about twenty-five feet away. I got in front of the toilet, and my legs gave out, sending me flying backwards, smashing my head on the hinge of the cabinet. I lay in a pool of blood for a few seconds, when my mom came in and found me. She dialed 911, and the ambulance carted me off to the hospital. Luckily, I was okay and only had a concussion.

My dad was absent at the time visiting his dad, who was dying of cancer. Papa, as I called him, was a genuine, hardheaded man who would give you the shirt off his back.

As a child, we would take trips to Texas to visit him and my grandma. I remember him reading my favorite storybook, *Suppertime For Frieda Fuzzy Paws*, to me because, like the kitten in the book, I often wanted to eat his delicious homemade chocolate chip cookies before dinner. Despite the distance between us, he, as well as my grandma, showered me with love and encouragement.

* * *

After I hit my head and my myasthenia worsened to the point that I couldn't really walk, my mom decided to take me back to the neurologist. She explained to her what was going on and that I had been gaining weight at the astonishing rate of twenty pounds per mouth. She told my mom that she shouldn't worry about the weight, that it would come off once the Prednisone was discontinued. She increased my Imuran and gave me instructions to start reducing the Prednisone. She also set up appointments for me to see a physical therapist and a dietician.

The physical therapist came to my house for an assessment. After she assessed me and decided that I needed a wheelchair, we had to borrow one from an organization until a new one was ready for me. I grew annoyed at the physical therapist, who clearly didn't understand my disease. Each time she saw me, she would just tell me to "walk this amount of stairs and then, the next day, double it." I could barely stand by myself, let alone climb stairs. I was a prisoner in my own house and rarely went out unless I had an appointment of some kind.

As we reduced the Prednisone, my weight not only remained but continued to climb at a steady pace. I now weighed about 230 pounds and was depressed and moody from the decrease of Prednisone. I was like a ten-year-old heroin addict going through withdrawal. I would call my mom, whom I loved dearly, a fucking bitch; two seconds later I'd be crying, and then smiling. I was scared and confused, and, at the same time, my disease wasn't getting any better.

* * *

It was now summertime, and Kristy had spent the entire summer at my house when her mom finally dragged her by her hair into the car, kicking and screaming. We had a lot of fun that summer. We rented movies, played games, and, on a good day, I'd walk down the stairs, and Kristy would push me in my wheelchair to the park behind our house.

We were the best of friends and made up our own song, equipped with a handshake similar to patty cake. We'd sing loud that so the entire neighborhood could hear us: "Kristy and Lauren are best friends, sugar and spice and everything nice! We are cool, and you are not. If you don't like it, shove it up your ass, your ass, your ass, ass, ass!" We were silly kids, but our friendship was anything but a joke.

This is my little brother, Bud, my sister, Amber, and me (age 10). This was taken in the house with stairs, and I was in a wheelchair.

* * *

Fall came, and it was time to go back to school. I was starting grade four, and many times I'd try to go, but, after flying downstairs, more 911 calls, and being so tired I could hardly move, my parents and I decided to switch me to hospital homebound schooling.

Twice a week, an older woman would come to teach me for an hour. We became close, and I grew fond of her. She told my parents that I was a gifted student and that she had a hard time challenging me, so we often finished early and played cards. A horse had fallen on my teacher, breaking both of her hips, so she knew what it was like to be sick and to spend time in the hospital. She understood how I felt, at least a little bit. Seeing that I was isolated in my house, she was able to get a computer donated to me. This gave me an outlet and a way to communicate with other people who were also sick. My mom had taken off work to take care of me, and we couldn't afford to move to a new house, which was what I needed.

At this point, I was off the Prednisone, taking only Imuran and Mestinon. My disease was still getting worse, and my mom took me back to the neurologist. After complaining of the weight gain and symptoms from my myasthenia, the neurologist increased the Imuran again and sent me to a dietician. She said that, in a few months, I should notice a difference and that the weight would began to come off.

✳ ✳ ✳

Over the next few months, I saw the dietician once a month. She suggested meal plans to me and put me on a twelve hundred calorie a day diet. I continued to see the neurologist each month, complaining of my weight and myasthenic symptoms, which were still out of control. Each time, she'd just listen and nod, sending me back home to the life I was beginning to hate. I was depressed, sick, bored, and trapped. I'd had enough, and seeing the neurologist, dietician, and physical therapist wasn't helping anything. Feeling like we were at a dead end, neither my parents nor I knew what to do.

After noticing the way I felt depressed and trapped in the house, my parents decided to move us to a new house, twenty minutes from the one we were living in at the time. It was a three-bedroom rancher and had no stairs. I would finally be able to live life outside my house and go places, something I couldn't do before.

I went back to see the neurologist and my mom told her that I was using a manual wheelchair to get around but was too tired and unable to push myself. She suggested getting an electric wheelchair and seeing the physical therapist again for an assessment. I saw the physical therapist, and I was fitted for an electric wheelchair. In the meantime, I used a loaner electric wheelchair, which was old and rickety. A few months later, they delivered the wheelchair, and I was ecstatic. With the new electric wheelchair, I could go out for longer periods of time. It gave me more freedom, since I couldn't walk.

Every few months, we'd return to the neurologist, but, after noting my increased symptoms and weight gain, she made no changes or suggestions. We decided to go back to see the pediatrician who initially diagnosed me, and, at this time, he suggested Intravenous Immunoglobulin therapy, also known as IVIG. IVIG would, hopefully, affect the function or the production of antibodies in the immune system. He admitted me to the hospital to do the treatment. They infused it through an IV for a couple hours. After seeing only slight improvement after the first round and none after the second round of IVIG, I returned home still taking Mestinon and a high dose of Imuran. I was still really sick, and we had adjusted our lives to my condition. We were beginning to think that this was "normal" and that there was no alternative for me. I continued to home school for the remainder of grade five and decided that, despite my illness, I would attempt to go back to school for grade six.

CHAPTER 6–
A CRUEL WORLD

Every day, or most days, I went to school. I put all of my frustration into my schoolwork and excelled in almost every subject. I worked very hard and settled for nothing but the best. The kids at school gave me mixed emotions. The kids who were in my class and knew me were very nice and helped me out if I needed to hand in assignments or get books.

The older kids in the other classes made fat comments or wheelchair jokes and bothered me at lunchtime. I was extremely hurt by this and was pushed to the point that I'd cry, which was hard to make me do from name-calling. I was a strong girl, but I was only human and could only take so much. I wanted the other kids to like me, and I couldn't understand how kids could be so cruel. Two older boys once tried to flip me over in my wheelchair during recess. I was still in no way a pushover, so I fought back by running over their feet until they left me alone.

But the problem wasn't just the kids. It was the adults who shocked me the most. I had been out of school in the hospital for about a week. After returning to school, I asked my teacher what was going on in that particular subject, and he replied, "Well, if you'd show up once in a while, you'd know!" Shocked and pissed off, disgusted at this grown man who should know better, I screamed back at him, "I was in the hospital!" All he could manage was a measly "oh." That's it. Not "I'm sorry" or any form of apology. Just "oh." Still angry about it, I decided to tell my dad, who went down to the school and threatened to "kick the shit out of him" if he ever spoke to me like that again. He was nice to me from that day forward.

When I was out anywhere, not just when I was at school, people would stare, snicker, or make rude gestures or comments. This usually angered Kristy or my sister, and they'd either tell them off or beat them up.

School was becoming increasingly hard for me, and the long days began to take a toll on my body, so it was brought to the school's attention that I would need an aide. The aide they provided for me wasn't very understanding and was very irritating to me. I'd ask her to help me with my jacket, and she'd say, "You did it earlier by yourself just fine. Do it yourself." She clearly didn't understand the nature of my disease and the way my strength fluctuated throughout the day.

I participated in the physical education class at my school, doing the very best I could do in all aspects of the subject. I would even play dodge ball in my wheelchair. Despite my efforts and the fact that I was in an electric wheelchair, my P.E. teacher decided to give me a C+. My mom phoned the principal and told them that this was absolutely ridiculous and that they were to either give me an A or no grade at all. After arguing with her about it, they finally decided to give me no grade at all.

I finished grade six that year with honor roll status, but, even though I liked being with the other kids, I just simply couldn't do it anymore. My disease was still getting worse and was completely out of control, and I was still gaining weight. The school couldn't meet my needs, and I was sick of it all.

CHAPTER 7-
COPING:
PROBLEMS ARISE

I started grade seven, and, like before, a teacher would come once a week, for an hour each time. Kristy had just moved fifteen minutes away from me, and almost every weekend we'd go to the mall, usually with my sister and her friends, and steal everything we could get our hands on. We'd come home, lay everything out on the bed and rummage through the stolen goods. We'd steal anything, CDs or movies, toys or make-up, everything we saw that we wanted. My parents eventually found all my stuff, and, although they were angry, they didn't say anything to me since I was so sick. Eventually we all got caught and stopped.

My parents, bogged down by stress, argued a lot. My dad was so bothered by my sickness that he'd sometimes pull over to the side of the road on his way to work and puke his guts up. My mom loved me dearly, but taking care of me everyday and catering to my every need, from showering to helping me onto the toilet, was taking a toll on her, physically and mentally. She started using drugs, and it seemed like she was always incoherent or angry. We tried talking to her about getting help, but that only made her distance herself from us more.

My parents weren't the only ones having problems. My sister was now a complete wreck. She had daily episodes and spent most of her time away from home and away from me. When she was around me, she usually picked on me, and we'd end up getting into fist fights. All attention was focused on me, and Amber was crying out to my parents for help, who had no time or energy for her. She became depressed, started doing drugs, and dropped out of school. Despite this, my sister and I still had a loving relationship. I didn't know exactly how to help her or what to say. All I knew was that my family went to hell in a handbasket, and I felt as though I was to blame.

* * *

I turned to Kristy in my time of need, and we began spending tons of time together. She would religiously come to my house from Friday to Sunday, every week. We'd sit in my bedroom, listening to rap music and singing along. We'd go for long strolls, exploring my neighborhood, and our adventures were priceless. We would play board games and card games, watch movies, and make our own *MADtv* skits.

We'd make cookies and cakes and get my brother to film us, pretending to do a cooking show. My brother, as the film director, would make hilarious comments during the show, usually dissing us, but we laughed at his comic personality anyway.

Kristy and I loved to eat all kinds of junk food and often had "feasts." Being with her, an extremely petite girl who could eat anything she wanted and not gain weight, made me feel like I was a regular kid, eating whatever I wanted, even though I was a 270-pound twelve-year-old.

Kristy and I did unusual things like going to an apartment complex to wipe out a whole population of snails or staying up all night on the computer on a voice chat, telling jokes and rapping to people. We'd go through the graveyard by my house at midnight, and we'd split up with walkie-talkies and try to scare each other. Being with Kristy was definitely a positive experience in my life, and, when we were together, we'd laugh so hard that we'd both forget I was sick.

In February, my grandpa, who had been battling cancer, lost his battle and sadly passed away. My dad flew to Texas for the funeral, and we all tried to stay strong for my dad.

My uncle Rodger, who adored me and to whom I was close, had a connection at the local paper. He put me in contact with the lady who wrote articles, and she did a short article on me, my illness, and the financial stress it placed on our family, which was struggling to make ends meet. The article was published around Christmas-time, and people donated a shower chair, a Nintendo with games, and some other random things to me after seeing the article. Around this time, my mom also raised money from various organizations for a wheelchair van, which we didn't have.

One person, after reading the article, called my mom and told her of an amazing neurologist who was the best doctor in the field of my disease, myasthenia gravis. My mom got the doctor's number and scheduled an appointment for me to see him in a few months.

My myasthenia was still slowly worsening, and I couldn't really walk or stand by myself. I had some difficulty swallowing and chewing and would often slur my words like a drunk person. I had double vision on a daily basis, and my eyes drooped so badly that it looked like I was sleeping when I wasn't.

* * *

I was still maintaining my grades when we suddenly heard the devastating news that my beloved uncle Rodger, whom I had nicknamed "Unk the Hunk," had died of a drug overdose. My mom, the youngest of her five siblings, was the closest to him, and she had seen him almost everyday. This hurt my mom, and everyone else, deeply. The only person she had to take care of her after she was sixteen when her mom died of cancer was Rodger. Her dad had abandoned them, and the rest of her siblings stayed with boyfriends, girlfriends, or friends.

Rodger was a positive force in our lives, and used his charismatic biker persona to raise money for a children's hospital. He had arranged for me to meet the rapper Coolio when he came to Vancouver, had cried at my bedside with my parents when I was in ICU, and now he was gone. Rodger had been diagnosed with melanoma cancer, and, after seeing his mother suffer a horrible death, he began using drugs until he died in April of 1998. After the tragic loss of her brother, my mom finally quit using drugs, and things at home got better.

* * *

It was finally time for me to see this top neurologist, so my parents took me to see him. When I met him, he turned out to be a cold, short man, with a thick French accent. After he evaluated me and my parents explained my history, he said that I'd need to start on another immunosuppressive called cyclosporine. I'd get a blood test once a month while on this drug, but he explained that its only side effects were that it increased hair growth and tasted awful.

Over the next few months, I finally started to see an improvement. I was better able to stand by myself, and the symptoms in my upper body had lessened. I was happy that things were improving, but I was still very sick, overweight, sad about Rodger's death and about missing out on so many things I'd wanted to do, like dance and play baseball.

I was a confused thirteen-year-old, and no one understood. So Kristy and I decided to try marijuana. We'd go up to the school and light up, then head over to Dairy Queen for a blizzard. We did this periodically, and then we stopped.

One day, on our way back home, high, Kristy and I saw a group of girls who had been mean to me in elementary school. They looked over, and one yelled a fat comment to me. Hearing this, Kristy chased her down the street and slapped her to the ground. She never bothered me again.

I finished grade seven that year with honor roll status yet again and decided that, in the fall, I'd try going to high school.

CHAPTER 8-
DESPERATE TIMES
CALL FOR DESPERATE
MEASURES

It was fall, and I had decided to try going to the high school by my house. I was taking on a regular schedule of classes, two of them being tutorial blocks during which I could work on my homework. This helped because it meant less work for me to do after school so that I could get some rest and not be a dead body the following day. At school, I hung out with my new friend, Earla. Her brothers hung around with my brother, so we became good friends and hung out when I wasn't with Kristy.

* * *

It was February, the day after Valentine's Day, and my sister was taking my brother and me to school. We were cruising casually down the street and had almost reached my school. The roads were clear and dry, and it was a nice, sunny day.

Out of nowhere, a blue Explorer sped out of his driveway, impacting his drivers side on our front end. We were going only 45 kilometers per hour, but that meant so was I. I flew forward into the back of my brother's seat, the metal part of my wheelchair slamming so hard into my legs that I began screaming that they were broken. I lay pinned between the heap of black medal and seat as I cried and screamed for somebody to unpin me and put me back in my chair, out of which I had half fallen.

My brother and sister, who were jammed into the dashboard and steering wheel, attempted to rescue me. My brother got out of the car and, still in shock, fell face first onto the ground. Some bystanders walking by opened the van door and pulled down the ramp. They picked me up and put me into the broken wheelchair. As tears streamed down my face, my sister yelled for someone to call an ambulance. My sister came around to me and helped me wheel down the ramp, out of the van, and off the road.

The ambulance arrived and loaded me onto a stretcher to transport me to the hospital. They checked out both my legs and, after taking an X-ray, found that, fortunately, I only had bad bruises. However, the emotional trauma would linger with all of us, every time we got into a car.

* * *

I went back to see my new neurologist, and he suggested sending me to a rehabilitation center for two months for weight loss and exercise. I don't think he fully understood my situation, that I didn't have enough physical strength to live without a wheelchair, but I agreed to do whatever was necessary to get better. So I left school for two months to visit a rehabilitation center in Vancouver.

Every day, I'd do as much exercise as my body would physically allow. We'd swim, take walks, use exercise machines, and play physical games. Each day, I'd see a dietician, physiotherapist, and psychologist, as well as teachers who could help me with my school work. I pushed myself to the very limit, which only seemed to set me back. Some days I couldn't even get out of bed. I was also put on a twelve hundred calorie a day diet.

I missed everyone terribly, especially Kristy. So she and I devised a plan to sneak her into the rehabilitation center, which wasn't allowed. There was an old, coffee-stained desk in my room that had six drawers for clothing and other personal items. Underneath, it was hollow, perfect for a secret sleeping spot. I put blankets over the opening with pictures and decorations a few days before Kristy was to come so that all the staff would see it beforehand and think nothing of it. Our plan went smoothly, and Kristy came that night and, after laughing and rekindling our friendship, she went to sleep on the spot.

There was one problem, though. The weekend staff consisted of totally different people than the weekday staff, who had already seen the contraption and laughed. The night nurse came in to check on me and glanced suspiciously at the decorative curtain. She pulled up the curtain and shone her flashlight right in Kristy's eyes, which were shut as she pretended to be asleep. Kristy smiled awkwardly. We were busted. She started to get mad at us and explained that Kristy had to leave. However, it was the middle of the night, and Kristy had no way to get back to her house, which was forty-five minutes away. The nurse generously escorted Kristy to the lounge, where she let her sleep until morning.

After six weeks, I was physically and mentally spent. I missed my family, especially my mom, having spent every day with her, twenty four hours a day, seven days a week, since I got sick. I decided to leave the rehabilitation center prematurely after barely effective six weeks. Feeling disappointed that, despite my efforts, the rehabilitation center couldn't "cure" me, I returned home and became depressed. I decided to put my negative feelings into my school work and writing. I published the first poem I ever wrote, and my English teacher even read it aloud to the class.

Stupidly, at the time I wasn't taking my cyclosporine properly, and, within a couple months, it showed. I was now missing a lot of school, depressed, weaker, a whopping 320 pounds and continuing to eat out of depression.

I returned to my neurologist, and we decided that something needed to be done about my weight. We arranged for me to be admitted to the hospital for a starvation diet. The plan was for me to eat fifty calories a day for three weeks and then to slowly increase the amount of calories to seven hundred calories a day over the remainder of the three weeks. I was happy and nervous to try it, assuming that I was going to lose a whole bunch of weight.

I left school again and was admitted to the eating disorder unit at the hospital. Daily, I saw a dietician, therapist, and physiotherapist. For the first week and a half, I was so incredibly hungry that I felt like a wild boar wanting to attack its prey, food being the prey. It was nothing I'd ever felt before. On top of the hardcore diet, the physiotherapist had me doing lots of exercise. From the afternoon to evening, I had music and art therapy with the art and music therapists. I loved to sing and often found myself singing the words to songs while the music therapist played piano or guitar.

As the next two weeks passed, I thought less and less about eating. They would normally send carrots or cucumbers, and I'd throw it in the garbage because I could no longer fathom the thought of eating without throwing up.

The mood swings and disorientation from not eating were enough to drive any sane person crazy. I would try to do my homework and end up doing the same questions repeatedly, forgetting I had ever done them. I'd get mad at my family and cry my eyes out, and then, ten seconds later, I'd smile like the Cheshire cat.

After the first two weeks of my starvation diet, my magnesium levels dropped very low, and it was given to me intravenously. I remember that, during and for a few hours afterwards, I'd feel so myasthenically weak that I felt I was paralyzed.

At the end of the difficult portion of the weight loss program, I had only lost a measly eighteen pounds. I was disappointed because most people who starved for three weeks would lose much more. Still, it was a loss, and I took it and ran with it. Over the next three weeks, my caloric intake was slowly raised to seven hundred calories a day, which I was to maintain at home. After six weeks had passed, I'd lost a total of twenty-one pounds. I was happier and sleeping better because of the anti-depressant the psychiatrist had prescribed for me. I was able to take short walks and exercise a bit.

When I returned back home, however, I found it incredibly difficult to stick to my diet plan and began taking diet pills to aid in my weight loss. They were dangerous, but they suppressed my appetite to the point that even the thought of food made me squirm. I starved myself for five days and then ate a tiny meal each day for the rest of the month after that, which helped me lose an additional twenty pounds. I weighed 280 pounds, which was the leanest I'd been in a while.

This is me in the rehabilitation center, on the bicycle.

I started to throw up the cyclosporine after taking it each time. I think that the starvation diet somehow changed my taste buds because I could no longer stomach it. After telling my neurologist that I was puking it up, we discontinued the drug. My parents eventually found out that I was taking these diet pills and flushed them down the toilet. Of course, I begged and screamed to keep them, but it was for my own good.

* * *

School was going well, and grade eight was coming to an end. Even though I had missed a lot of school, I still managed to acheive honor roll status, over which I was beaming with pride.

The summer came and went and now, without the cyclosporine, I had gotten worse again. My chewing, swallowing, and slurring had come back to haunt me. I could no longer take short walks, my eyes drooped and had double vision, and my ability to move around had become sluggish.

I decided to return to school for grade nine anyway. This time, Kristy would attend the same school as I did for the first time. We got our schedules to discover that we were in English and Science together. School started, and every day Kristy would wake up at the crack of dawn to take the bus to school, which was pretty far from her house. School went well, and I maintained good grades even though I felt crappy.

Kristy and I were so rowdy in class that we often got moved away from each other, which didn't stop us. We'd fly paper airplanes notes to each other or make faces from across the room. Kristy was a great friend and would stick up for me when the kids threw something, like an apple or a slushee, at the back of my wheelchair or call me names, like "Jabba the Hut" or "cripple." It drove Kristy nuts to see people treating me so badly, and that often lead to arguments or fist fights.

For my fifteenth birthday, Kristy put an announcement on the school's television station, which was in all the classes, saying: "Happy 15th Birthday, Lauren! Love, Kristy!" It had a picture of Winnie the

Pooh hugging Tigger, and, when I saw it, I got teary eyed.

After my birthday, I put back on all the weight I'd lost and then some. My disease was still picking at me, so I went back to see my neurologist. He suggested another immunosuppressant called Cellcept. I immediately started taking it, and, as the months passed, saw no improvement.

Meanwhile, Kristy and I were having a blast at school. On the days she slept at my house, we almost never went or would show up late. Eventually, the school had to change Kristy's schedule, and she was transferred out of both of my classes. To make up for lost time, we found ourselves skipping most afternoon blocks and either going to a restaurant to eat or wandering around, exploring. The school year came to an end, and I once again pulled honor roll status out of my hat, despite the amount of missed days.

That summer, my dad, my brother, and I decided to drive to Texas to visit my grandma and relatives. We even stopped at Yosemite National Park along the way to see the geysers. My brother and I had a lot fun together; we'd do crazy things and often found ourselves in trouble, just like Kristy and me, like the time when we decided to walk

This is my dad, my grandma, my cousin, my brother, and me in Texas in the summer of 2001.

a mile to the convenience store in 114 degree heat or when we decided to have a "fruit fight" with my grandma's fake antique fruit basket. After spending a couple of weeks with my grandma, aunts, and cousins, we returned home.

* * *

The summer came to a halt, and a new fresh school year started. Kristy's mom now wanted her to go to the same school as her younger sister, Holly, which was closer to their house, so I went back to school for grade ten, sad and alone. My disease was steadily taking over, and I found myself only going to school for half days. I was struggling to finish my courses, even though we were only focusing on three: English, Socials and Science.

I went back to see my neurologist, complaining of my symptoms and horrible quality of life. He told me that he would admit me to the hospital where I'd have a line inserted for plasmapheresis. We would also arrange to try IVIG again.

It was the day before my sixteenth birthday, and the line was traumatically inserted in the catheter lab. It was a very painful experience for me. What was supposed to be a twenty-minute procedure turned into two of the longest hours of my life. I was lying there, my breast exposed for the world to see, crying compulsively, with sky-blue plastic drapes covering my head. Embarrassed, petrified, and so nervous that I thought I'd shit myself, I lay there shaking nervously as he searched for the vein close to my heart. I still remember the intense burning I felt because the area was not fully numbed. As I clenched down, the vein suddenly popped up, and the surgeon began pulling and tugging the line vigorously into my neck.

After it was over, I was physically and mentally drained. The next morning was my sixteenth birthday. The sounds of suffering woke me up in the emergency room at about six in the morning. I lay there in bed, unable to move my neck, and then it hit me like a ton of bricks. I burst into tears realizing it was my sweet sixteen, and there was nothing sweet about it. I was so done.

They moved me to a room that day, and my family came equipped with cake, flowers, and balloons. Kristy arrived that evening with two knapsacks filled with clothing and necessities. She was out of school for spring break and was going to stay with me for the rest of my time in the hospital. She asked the nurse for a rollout bed, wedged it into the corner of my room, and got comfortable. The fun had begun, and Kristy was there to lift my spirits.

I had plasmapheresis two days in a row, then skip two days before doing plasmapheresis three more times. I felt great because of the treatment and had no trouble chewing, swallowing, talking, or breathing. I could even walk fifty feet at one time as well as do some exercises.

During that spring break, Kristy and I had a lot of fun; you wouldn't think you could have that much fun in the hospital. One night, we crept down to the basement. It was after midnight, and I was pulling Kristy around in a manual wheelchair with my electric wheelchair. We got out of the elevator and continued down a long, dark, hallway until we reached a sign that read "Morgue."

Horrified, we both looked at each other wide-eyed and took off down the hallway. Kristy ditched the wheelchair, stood up, and began running. To stop her from leaving me, I grabbed her by the back of her baggy pajama pants and pulled. Down came her pants, exposing her entire bottom on camera. As she kept running, she pulled them up, and we began laughing hysterically. She got another wheelchair by the elevator, and we got in and went up a few floors. I was pulling her at top speeds around sharp corners, when we noticed a security guard chasing us.

"Faster! He's on our ass! He's on our ass!" Kristy screamed with amusement.

We sped into the doctor's lounge and shut the door. Phew, we lost him. The next day, Kristy and I got a bright idea—deflate all fourteen of my helium balloons and talk like chipmunks. Kristy took out her tape recorder, and we sat in the lounge singing like midgets from the *Wizard of Oz.*

Later that night, Kristy and I were looking through magazines, cutting out words for the collage we were making. The nurse came in and hooked up my IVIG treatment through my catheter. As we sat there looking through magazines, Kristy suddenly looked up and yelled, "Holy shit! You look like a tomato!"

I felt sweaty and hot, and my throat began to swell, making it hard for me to breathe. Panicked, Kristy ran for the nurse, and within seconds they returned, stopping my IVIG treatment. Within a few minutes, my face and throat returned to normal. The nurse went to talk to the doctor, and he explained to her (and she, in turn, explained to me) that it was an allergic reaction and that we would not be able to continue with the treatment.

* * *

The following day, my neurologist and his team of colleagues came to see me. They said that I'd be having plasmapheresis weekly to keep me functioning and that we would start another immunosuppressant called Prograf.

I went back home and, over the next few months, my disease continued to get worse. I decided to discontinue both the Cellcept and Prograf, as it seemed that they weren't helping after several months. It seemed as though the disease was now focusing more on my upper extremities, including swallowing, breathing, chewing, and talking. Despite the weekly plasmapheresis, I couldn't really take more than a few steps and could only transfer by myself. I could no longer go to school and decided to transfer back to hospital homebound to complete Socials, English, and Science 10. I finished my courses with honor roll standing and continued to see Kristy on weekends, and then it happened.

Years of taking care of me and watching me suffer had finally destroyed my mom emotionally. Our roles reversed, and now I watched the loving, chatty, extroverted, fight-for-your-rights woman I once knew suffering from extreme depression and psychosis. She became withdrawn, talked to plants, heard voices, saw things that weren't there, and rambled on about government conspiracies, hackers, and doctors trying to kill me. She stopped smoking, eating, and became a totally different person. We tried to get my mom the help she needed, but she wouldn't go to the doctors. There was nothing to be done but sit and watch in disbelief.

I no longer wanted to be around her although I knew she was sick, and I felt bad for wanting to get away because I knew it was all my fault. Kristy was there for me that summer and helped to take my mind off my mom. I was still having plasmapheresis weekly, and, as the months passed, my mom was getting worse.

It was a stifling hot summer day when the showdown that would save my mom happened. She went nuts on my sister, punched her in the face, and then began screaming that my sister had attacked her. She had invented the scenario in her paranoid, confused mind. My sister and I saw this as an opportunity to get her help, so we called 911 and had them come and take her to the hospital. She stayed for just over a week, and the doctors treated her for depression and psychosis. She came home and was doing well. The mom I knew and loved had returned.

✳ ✳ ✳

A new school year began, and a teacher came out to see me twice a week. It was the middle of September, and I began having chills, fever, diarrhea, and extreme weakness. When I went for my plasmapheresis that week, they discovered that the line was infected and admitted me to the hospital.

The infection was running rampant through my blood, so they started me on some heavy duty antibiotics and hoped for the best. They gave me two plasmapheresis treatments to give me some strength, and, to my surprise and the doctor's, my body rid itself of the infection in a shocking five days. My immune system was obviously not suppressed enough.

They removed my infected line and told me that I'd need a new one inserted. Remembering the traumatic experience from the first line, I stupidly declined. I returned home with no line, taking no treatment but Mestinon, which could only do so much. I was depressed, and I'd had enough. My myasthenia was now controlling my life, and I was letting it.

CHAPTER 9- THE BEST BIRTHDAY EVER

On my seventeenth birthday, my family, Kristy, and I would be going on a cruise. It had been a rough year for all of us, and we desperately needed a break. We drove to California in our wheelchair van. We had all of our stuff packed and stacked at the very back of the van. My mom and Kristy had made little blanket nests on the floor around my wheelchair. I stretched out on the bench seat with pillows and blankets. My brother sat up front with my dad to keep him company while he drove. The van was a huge mess with stuff scattered everywhere; it reminded me of a messy frat house.

We arrived in California after a long but hilarious twenty-five-hour drive. We stayed in a decent hotel, which was pure luxury compared to what we were used to. We had never been on a cruise and couldn't wait for the following day to board the boat.

That night, Kristy and I awoke at three a.m., hyper and laughing hysterically. We woke my brother with all our excitement, and he, too, joined in the fun. We were being loud and cracking jokes and eventually woke my parents. My parents were so excited themselves that they stayed up and couldn't go back to sleep.

Kristy and I got ready, fixed our hair and make up and decided to go get some breakfast. We wandered down the road from the hotel in downtown California until we found a convenience store. We got a box of doughnuts and some hot chocolate and headed back to our hotel while harassed by the early morning crackheads, who picked at us like baby birds biting at worms. We found this pretty creepy but humorous.

The hours passed slowly, but it was finally time to head to the boat to check in. We left the hotel, arrived, parked our van, and put our luggage onto a cart. After two hours of waiting and checking in, we walked across a long platform into the huge boat. The inside carpet was a deep red background with multicolored squiggly lines. It was fun, yet elegant and plush, and complimented the golden colored walls. We were greeted by workers from different countries. Our eyes were wide with excitement as they directed us to the glass elevators, leading upwards to the top deck.

We stepped out onto the deck to hear Bob Marley's "Jammin" playing. There was a huge arrangement of food awaiting us. There was a huge pool and hot tub equipped with a slide. The sky was blue, clear, and sunny, and we felt like we were on a huge, floating tropical paradise. We sat down, stuffing our faces with an assortment of food from the buffet. We then went down the elevator to check out our room. It was a small, cramped room with bunk beds, which didn't bother Kristy and me at all since we'd hardly be sleeping, anyway.

Each day, Kristy and I would wake up, get ready, eat a huge breakfast, and then do all the fun activities and see all the shows the boat had to offer. If there was ever a dull moment, we'd either eat, tan, or get drunk. At dinner time, we'd dress up in elegant clothes and go to the nice dinner which served gourmet food. We enjoyed the experience of 'feeling rich' and trying new things.

Our boat set sail for Catalina Island and Ensenada, Mexico. The following day, we came to Catalina Island, where I found that I was unable to bring my electric wheelchair on the tenders to cross to the island. Saddened, I stayed on the boat with Kristy, while everyone else got off. Kristy and I got really drunk that day and burned to a crisp.

The next day was my birthday, and I awoke to discover I looked like a monster. My face was bright red, swollen, and scabbed. My eyes were sunk back in my head from the swelling. There was no way that I was going to let this stop me from enjoying my vacation, so I threw on a pair of glasses and took off. That day, we had a birthday cake for me, and the whole restaurant sang to me. We watched the comedian and the dance shows in the theater and had an excellent time. It was the best birthday ever.

The next day we arrived in Mexico. We got up early and got off the boat. It was a small little town with lots of people and lots of shops. Kristy and I separated from my family and took off on our own. Scavenging through the boutiques for souvenirs and deals, we came across a hair braider. In the middle of the street, the old Mexican lady began braiding my long, thick, curly hair. She had her child in a knapsack dangling from her back. Kristy went inside a shop while I sat in the sun, getting my hair braided.

When she returned, my hair was in beautiful braids, and I had been sitting for about twenty minutes getting acquainted with some random Spanish guy who had come over to chat me up. He ended up staying with us the entire day, protecting us from the thugs that roamed the downtown area. We taught him English words, and, in return, he spoke Spanish to the people in the town to get us good deals. As night fell, we said goodbye to our friend and exchanged addresses. He walked us to the boat and then left us. We watched from the top deck of our boat as fireworks went off and the boat pulled off and went on its way back to California. Our cruise came to an end, and, the next day, we left on our long drive home.

Mom, Dad, Bud, and me getting ready to go have dinner on the boat.

CHAPTER 10- BEING A TEENAGER

I had finished that school year with a measly two courses under my belt, English and Socials 11. I had an A in English and a B in Socials. Although it wasn't a lot, it was what I could physically handle for the time being. My disease was still progressing, and I was becoming more and more depressed.

I started smoking marijuana again that summer with my two buddies, Kristy and Holly. We'd sneak off to the school or bushes to get high. We would usually smoke pot and then walk up to the grocery store to get munchies. One day, we stopped to look at a dead bunny that was lying in the shoulder of the road. We crept up close, and, just then, a car came speeding by, running over the bunny and splashing its guts all over us. We ran screaming all the way back to my house.

Once we were cruising down the shoulder of a busy road. It was ten o'clock at night, and Kristy was standing on the back of my wheelchair, hanging on for dear life as we sped down the jagged hill. Out of nowhere, a huge eighteen-wheeler semi pulled up to us, and the driver began yelling obscenities at us and telling us to "pull over." Ignoring him, assuming he was crazed, we continued speeding down the hill, laughing so hard we couldn't talk. We sped up to try to lose him, each time laughing harder, as Kristy's head was level with his window. He crazily tried to run us off the road as Kristy yelled that the headlights were so hot that they were burning her ass. We finally took a sharp turn off the road and onto the grass where the crazy man followed. We couldn't believe it; he was driving a huge eighteen-wheeler through grass and bushes! We turned sharply down my street, finally losing him. Realizing that we could have been killed while all this was happening oddly made Kristy and me only laugh harder. We had many adventures and fun-filled times that summer.

One particular day, near the end of the summer, Kristy and I had decided to go downtown and smoke pot at a pot-smoking café. After smoking a couple of joints, a random guy named Jerry came over to us and started chatting. We started talking with him as he smoked a joint with us. In joined another guy, Rocky, who we thought was Jerry's friend at the time. Two other English guys joined in, Ash and Martin. We all gathered around and sat down at a table. Matching joints, we sat talking and laughing for two hours. We rambled on about the weird surfer paintings on the wall, which now appeared vivid and real, and how red everyone's eyes were.

We started to notice that Rocky was shaking and sniffling and was, in general, acting really weird. Jerry announced he didn't know Rocky at all and then it dawned on us. He didn't know him at all; Rocky was just some random crackhead from downtown smoking up everyone else's weed, while he sat and pretended to roll a joint.

Kristy and I looked at each other, looked back at him, and then our eyes met again. We, being extremely ripped and paranoid, stared at each other wide-eyed like it was the end of the world. Kristy suddenly flew up out of her seat and announced, "Good thing we have that knife in case someone tries to follow us. Wouldn't wanna have to stab someone." She paused. "Again."

They all stared at us as if we were completely nuts. Kristy let out an awkward laugh and said, "Just joking." They sat there silently, still staring at us. We told them we were leaving and then bounced out the door.

It was eleven-thirty at night, and we were starving, so we wandered aimlessly downtown searching for a Subway. After thirty minutes of walking in circles, we realized that we had passed the Subway two times and finally entered the establishment. We shoveled   foot long sandwiches and chocolate chip cookies into our mouths. We got back on the skytrain and went home, where we passed out.

*   *   *

The new school year started, and I had signed up for a new online school. I began taking Biology 11 and Career and Personal Planning 11 and 12. I wanted to become a doctor, so I knew that I had to do well in biology.

It was October, 2003, I was 17 years old, and my mom, Kristy, Kristy's mom, and I would all be going on a cruise together. The second cruise would be even better then the first. We took a train, which was truly a trip from hell. The room Kristy and I shared was about six by nine feet. It had a toilet and bunk beds. Because it was a handicapped room, it was on the bottom floor above the wheels and shook violently like a roller coaster ride. Kristy and I had exactly two Gravol each to take so that we could sleep, which was nearly impossible. The train ride was scenic and beautiful, and we took tons of pictures out the window. It was a grueling thirty-six-hour train ride of puking and gut-wrenching shaking.

We finally arrived, and we checked into our hotel. I was very weak and exhausted from the trip and was completely dreading the trip back. We boarded the shuttle bus to our boat and found ourselves being driven at 100 miles an hour by a crazy Russian. We were holding on for dear life as he swerved in and out of traffic. He finally came to a sharp halt at our drop off and handed us our luggage.

We headed for the cruise check-in. It was a beautiful, sunny day, and we enjoyed the warmness as we fought our way through the crowds. As we got on the boat, we were greeted by the cruise workers. The boat was even bigger and more luxurious than our last one had been. We found ourselves, once again, on the top deck, experiencing the tropical paradise as the boat set sail for Mexico. This time, we'd be going to Puerto Vallarta, Mazatlan, and Cabo San Lucas.

We were thrilled. We visited all the shows, dances, and talent shows the boat had to offer. We tanned each day, and the four of us pretty much stayed drunk the entire duration of the cruise, which was seven days. We gambled in the casino like addicts, even though Kristy and I weren't old enough. At night, we'd all order room service and stay up laughing and chatting, watching Jay Leno.

We arrived in Puerto Vallarta, which had extremely high sidewalks that I couldn't get onto. So we ended up running down the streets of Mexico in the hundred degree heat , dodging traffic. We found a huge department store and wandered around. Realizing that there were no taxis that could carry my electric wheelchair, we returned to the boat, disappointed.

Kristy, my mom, and Kristy's mom left to go explore Puerto Vallarta, and I stayed on the boat. After a while my mom came back to find me upset and crying. My disease had once again ruined my life. My mom helped me into my pajamas and I went to sleep.

The next day, we arrived in Mazatlan. They had trolley carts with ramps that held my wheelchair. We went to town, and the gang and I browsed around the shops. We got our hair braided and then got a table by the bar to embark on our journey of alcohol. After five Mexican chi chis each, Kristy and I began dancing and singing loudly with some random people.

It was time to return to the boat, and Kristy and I were piss-tank drunk. We went up to our rooms and got ready for dinner. Kristy and I, along with our moms, sat down, and, within minutes, our heads were in the plates, nearly passed out. I felt a gurgle , exclaiming suddenly that I "just had to go." I flew out of the restaurant to the elevators and puked all over myself and the metal ashtray. My mom ran out behind me and took me up to our room to help me shower and change. I told her I was sorry, and I got into bed and passed out. Meanwhile, Kristy had, for some odd, drunken reason, crawled up the entire five staircases to her room. She eventually passed out. Our moms went off and left us to sleep it off.

We arrived in Cabo San Lucas the next day only to discover that I couldn't even get off the boat because they had tenders, which weren't equipped to carry my electric wheelchair. I wasn't strong enough, even with help, to step onto the little boat, so I insisted that they go without me. I didn't want to be the reason they missed out on such a beautiful place. I got into bed, depressed, and slept the rest of the afternoon. We enjoyed the rest of the cruise, and it came to an end as we pulled into the LA harbor. We caught the train from hell back home, and, thirty-six hours later, we arrived.

My good friend, Holly, and me at the mall's photo booth.

Kristy and me getting drunk on the boat one hot, sunny day.

Me on the boat, getting all 'elegant' for dinner
with my bubbly and Louie Vuitton bag.

CHAPTER 11-
THE NEGLECT THAT ALMOST ENDED IT ALL

When I came back from the cruise, I was really depressed. I was 17 years old, and my disease was at the worst it had ever been. I was receiving no treatment except Mestinon. I think part of the reason I got so depressed was the trip to Mexico. It was such a happy time, and now I had to come back to this. I wasn't in school, and, although I had Kristy and my family, I felt isolated and alone. I had no energy for anything and sat in my pajamas all day listening to music or playing computer solitaire. I was a strong girl. I had been through a lot. But physically and mentally, I was shutting down.

I always slept close to the edge of the bed, which was against the wall, next to a baseboard heater. It was winter so the heater was set on high. I must have been having a bad dream, because I somehow rolled into the crack between the bed and wall, where the heater was, and it started to burn into my flesh.

I awoke to feel myself burning, and I started screaming for help. My door was closed, and the room was pitch black. I was screaming, but no one could help me. I was too weak to wedge myself out of the crack, and I lay there crying, praying to God that someone would come in. Two minutes of burnt flesh later, my brother entered and came to my rescue. He rolled me back into my bed, and, in shock, I told him I'd had a bad dream. Then it hit me like a thousand knives stabbing. My arm. The pain. I started screaming, "Oh my God, something's wrong with my arm!"

He flipped on the light and gasped as he saw the dangling, skin from my entire arm. "What's wrong, what is it?" His jaw dropped, but he said nothing. He ran out of the room and came back with my dad.

"Oh, my God, how did this happen?" My dad screamed.

I was crying so hard that I was barely able to mutter a word. The pain was so intense and throbbing that I just wanted to amputate my arm. He covered me in aloe vera and bandages and gave me some Tylenol, which did little to ease the pain. Over time, my burn began to heal, and I tried to forget all the bad things that had happened to me, but that was impossible.

✻ ✻ ✻

I'd smoke pot with Kristy and Holly on weekends, and I had finished Biology and Career and Personal Planning with A's. I stopped doing my school work after that. I could no longer function, so I dragged myself back to my neurologist. When he saw me, he could tell by my mood and tone of voice that I was depressed and really sick. He once again suggested Prednisone, but, scared of mood swings, weight gain, and all the side affects that came along with it, I mistakenly declined. He suggested I go to California for a second opinion from another myasthenia specialist. I agreed and went back home. With each passing day, I was back to the beginning, as sick as I had been when I was first diagnosed, slowly dying.

January came, and it was time to go to California to get a second opinion. Kristy came with me, and my dad drove us in the van. I had been taking diet pulls again for about two months and had lost about 25 pounds. On top of that, I had the flu and didn't eat or sleep the whole twenty-five hour trip down. Kristy and I still managed to have fun, despite my obvious depression and sickness. About eight hours into the trip, my dad began getting sleepy and swerving a bit at the wheel. A cop saw this and pulled us over. Kristy and I were in the back with our headphones on pretending to be asleep, laughing and squinting at each other.

We finally arrived in Sacramento, where this specialist was located. That night, I was so sick that I just lay in the hotel bed, puking and shaking with a fever and chills. I was unable to swallow my Mestinon that day or night. The next day, I was still not improving, and we got in the car and headed to my appointment. After examining me and pondering for a second, he said one phrase I definitely didn't want to hear.

"You need Prednisone."

My heart sank. Angered and upset, I left his office and got into our van. I leaned my weak body on the back of my dads seat and started crying. This was my life now. More medication and more weight gain. I wondered if I was ever going to be normal. What was normal, anyway? I could hardly remember; it had been too long.

As I sobbed uncontrollably, the saliva in my throat began to thicken. Uh oh. Too late. My gut turned, and I began puking. As tears and puke rolled down my face, staining my blue pajama top, my chest heaved, and I searched for a breath. The thick saliva was now pouring out of my mouth as I began to panic. Kristy began pulling it out of my mouth to help clear my airway as my dad frantically searched for a medical supply store to get a turkey baste. He went inside a department store and returned with the manual suction. He attempted to suction my mouth, but it was no use. Things were getting bad fast, and my panic was only making the crisis worse. I puked on a towel that Kristy was using to wipe my mouth and began gurgling.

"Hospital," I mumbled through the thick goo.

As my neck fell backwards lifelessly, I began choking and suffocating. My dad and Kristy were both frazzled as they searched for the emergency room sign we'd seen earlier by the neurologist's office.

Kristy put her hands into my throat to try to clear the saliva. I watched her bug eyed and shaking as I gurgled the word "hurry." I knew things were bad, and, after I had ignored my illness for so long, it had come to claim me for the second time. After what seemed like forever but was only about two minutes, we found the hospital. My dad drove my electric wheelchair inside the building. I was not even able to hold my head up. It fell to the side, and I felt as though I was losing consciousness.

"We need help!" my dad yelled. He told the nurse that I was having a myasthenic crisis and needed my mouth suctioned immediately. The nurse ignored his request and attempted to take my temperature.

My dad screamed at her. "She needs her mouth suctioned, she can't breathe, she's going to die!"

Finally, the nurse directed us to a suction and hooked it up, and my dad began suctioning my throat. My dad told her what had happened and the events leading up to it. The nurse left to get a doctor, and, as the thick saliva was being suctioned from my mouth, I knew I was still in serious trouble. It was only a matter of time before I suffocated. I was scared and confused as I kept the suction in the back of my throat.

As we waited for a doctor, my dad said that he would go move the van, which he had left with Kristy in the no parking zone, and that he'd be back in a few minutes. Kristy came in and sat down on the stretcher next to me. Unable to talk, I let out a deep sigh, and Kristy looked at me, still shaking from the car ride from hell. The doctor came over, and, as I was unable to talk, Kristy explained to the woman what had happened. She knew me so well that she was even able to tell the doctor my Mestinon dosage and medical history.

The doctor said that I'd need to be admitted. Scared and still thinking unclearly, I told her I was fine and would stay a few hours then leave. She was hesitant and didn't want to let me leave, for obvious reasons. Two minutes later I started puking again, this time with blood in it. The doctor took one look at it and said, "You aren't going anywhere."

The nurse took my vital signs and some blood, and the respirator therapist did a force vital capacity to see how bad my breathing actually was. After blowing a horrible .6 liters, I got scared, knowing that they intubate if you blow under .8 liters. A few minutes later, the head ICU doctor and his team came to see me. I was in denial but already aware of my situation as he explained to me that they'd need to intubate me so that I could rest. He told me how dangerous the situation was and that, if we didn't intubate me soon, it might be too late.

Deathly afraid and homesick, I told him that I wasn't going to be intubated and that I could still breathe. He told me that, the minute it got too bad and he thought I needed it, they'd intubate me, anyway. He and his team left the room to talk to my dad outside the door.

As I lay in the small emergency room bed, a male nurse came in to insert a catheter into my bladder. I requested a female nurse, but he rudely told me that there was no one else available. As I was a seventeen-year-old girl and he was a young man who didn't look a day over 20, I lay there nervous and scared with my bottom half exposed. I asked him if it was going to hurt. He curtly replied "no" and jammed it in. I let out a swift, loud scream, and, as soon as he left, I burst into tears.

I sat alone for a few minutes, then the nurse came in and attempted to put in a feeding tube. She asked me if I was bulimic, and, when I shook my head "no," she began to insert the tube up my nose and into my stomach. It traumatized my nose, and I cried for her to stop as my nose began to bleed. She stopped and left the room.

My breathing was getting really bad, and I was petrified. As I struggled to breathe, I called for my dad. He came in, and I whispered, "Intubate now!" He ran outside the room and told the doctors that it was getting bad and that I needed to be intubated. After I had told him many times that I'd rather die than be intubated, my dad knew the seriousness of my decision and that, if I'd finally given in, it meant it was almost too late.

The doctors were getting set up, and, as I nervously waited, I could feel my chest getting heavier, like someone was sitting on it while I was trying to breathe. Within fifteen minutes, they were ready to intubate me. They explained that they'd spray my throat to numb it and that then they'd send a little camera down with the tube into my lungs. He told me that I should stay calm and that they were going to take care of me. I started to calm down, realizing that it was only a matter of minutes before the torture stopped.

He sprayed my throat, and I felt nothing as he inserted the tube into my lungs. I struggled slightly as I felt it moving around in my chest. I made a noise, and he told me to hang in there as he was almost done. Voila! It was in, and I felt a rush of air. Finally, I could breathe. The relief was soothing, and I gave a thumbs-up to the doctors and staff.

As I lay in the bed, I suddenly felt a warm presence standing behind me embracing me with love. It was a bold, strong presence that felt like Rodger and Papa. They had come to guide me through my time of need, and, at that moment, I knew I was going to be fine.

After that, they gave me some morphine and Versed so that I wouldn't remember the traumatic events. They gave me five plasmapheresis treatments over the next eleven days. I remember waking up for only a few minutes or seconds at a time. I remember seeing pictures and colors.

I would write things like "orange fuzzy monster" or "Take it out!" in angry scribbles, referring to the respirator I was on. I'd write other random, humorous things, like "Double cheeseburger with milkshake, please!" and "I'll take you out for dinner and buy you a present," referring to my dad's birthday, which was February 1st and was now ruined. I'd also write, "Where am I? What happened? Am I on a train?" Then my dad would explain for the hundredth time where I was and what happened.

Kristy came to visit me for about an hour each day for the first four days, but it was too difficult for her to see me lying there lifelessly. The doctors had told them both that I'd continue to dwindle and would probably die. Realizing this, my dad decided to send Kristy home on the greyhound. He sent Kristy on her way and checked out of the hotel. He went to a shelter where he could stay cheaply because he had a sick kid.

On the eleventh day, I opened my eyes, finally awake and pretty confused as to what had happened. My dad again explained it to me. He was happy to see me awake and doing better. The doctors came in to see me, and they said that, in a couple of days, they could get the tube out and maybe move me to another floor. Three days later, they removed the ventilator, and I breathed on my own. It felt good, and I breathed with ease. While I was asleep for those eleven days, they had started me on a high dose of Prednisone.

The head ICU doctor was very kind and said he had a special private room with the most beautiful view of downtown Sacramento ready and waiting for me. For the next week, I stayed all day with my dad, feeling much better. My dad and I would play cards and watch TV together. I asked him things I never knew about him, abut his life and what kind of music he loved. We got closer, and I could tell that he was ecstatic to see me doing better instead of dying like the doctors had said.

The night before I was supposed to go home, I was having another plasmapheresis treatment. At the very end of it, I began feeling like I was going to pass out. I lost consciousness and was unresponsive for a couple minutes. They got me into the bed and called a code blue. My blood pressure had dropped to 70 over 35. As people came in with the crash cart, I opened my eyes and looked around. It looked like I was in a room filled with diamonds or mirrors everywhere. I started to feel a bit better. I drank some water, and they said they'd give me some fluids overnight to bring up my blood pressure.

The next day, a surgeon came to see me and notified me that, while I was "asleep," they had done a CAT scan of my chest. The CAT scan revealed that my thymus gland, which I had once had removed, had grown back. They wanted me to stay and have surgery to remove it, but I was doing much better and told the doctors that I'd be going home. We left that afternoon, and I sat up front with my dad the whole way home.

73

CHAPTER 12 - BRINGING ON THE HEARTBREAK

After returning home from my unexpected three-week hospital stay, I unpacked my stuff, slid into my jammies, and cozied up to my mom on her rose-patterned king size bed. My sister, her husband, and my brother all rushed in to see me. We told the long story of my triumph over my body. Once again, I had surprisingly pulled through, despite my odds. My family was glad to have me back and showered me with love.

The next day, Holly and Kristy came over for our long-awaited reunion bearing gifts, my old green friend, marijuana. They were thoughtful friends; they knew that I had just been through a huge ordeal and were happy to be the ones to numb my pain. They came to my house, met me with hugs and homemade cards, the best kind.

I explained my recovery to them, and Kristy told me all about her interesting twenty-five hour bus ride home. I knew she was scared that I was going to die because, despite the long ride with no food or sleep, she came home and, instead of going to sleep, got drunk until she puked. Had the roles of been reversed, I probably would have done the same thing.

We got high and laughed so hard that night. They were surprised at how easily I could dismiss everything that had happened to me. Every weekend after that for the next four months, we'd hang out and get stoned, each time more than before.

I went to see my neurologist, and he put me back on Cellcept. I had plasmapheresis every week and remained on 80mg of Prednisone daily until April, when it was reduced to 50mg a day. I found that, between the heavy duty pot smoking and the high dose Prednisone, I was packing on the pounds rapidly. I left the hospital in California at 302lbs and was now at 335lbs.

My 18th birthday came, and Kristy, Holly, my family, a few others, and I celebrated. We had cake and dinner, and then my friends and I topped off the night with eighteen joints.

My face had now swelled so much that the bottom of my chin was huge and covered in stretch marks. I felt like my face was ruined, and I didn't even look like myself anymore. My feet were also swollen and covered with stretch marks, and I had excruciating pain in my joints.

I went back to my neurologist, and we decided to reduce the Prednisone which was causing this terrible pain and swelling. We also reduced the Cellcept and would start another immunosuppressant called Cytoxan, which is also used for chemotherapy. It would substitute for the reduction of Prednisone, from which I was feeling weaker. I went into the hospital for a day for the infusion of Cytoxan. I came home with a headache, feeling tired, and went to sleep.

I had been sleeping long 15- to 18-hour days but didn't think too much of it until I started having trouble breathing every time I moved. I would get up to go to the bathroom and feel like I was suffocating. I was getting low fevers, and, when I mentioned my difficulty breathing to my doctor, he thought that it might be related to my obesity.

Despite feeling bad, a few days later I decided to go play bingo with my mom and Kristy. That night I remember joking, "I probably have pneumonia." But, really, I wasn't joking. Subconsciously I knew, and I was serious. Dead serious. I started coughing that night, and it only got worse throughout the night. By the next day, my breathing was so shallow that I couldn't move. I had a raging fever, and my myasthenia was in full effect. I was sitting at the kitchen table, my guts turning at the thought of being intubated again.

My parents finally convinced me to let them take me to the hospital. My parents talked to the nurse, and they brought me to the ICU emergency room section. The head ICU doctor came down, and, like before, I sat there trying to convince him and myself that I didn't need intubation. That was a lie, and I was in denial once again, only this time I was in too deep. I had waited so long that it would almost be too late. They took an X-ray and gave me the diagnosis: pneumonia. They pumped some antibiotics into me, and my stomach began to churn. I started to feel even weaker, and I was tired of breathing and coughing. I knew it was only a matter of time.

"We have no choice, you're a beautiful young girl and we want to keep you that way." The neurologist cooed with the ICU doctor. I agreed, requesting only that I feel no pain. As the anaesthesiologist and doctors prepared for the intubation, the ICU doctor pushed me in my wheelchair to the operating room.

"We have to hurry; it's getting worse," I was barely able to whisper.

They had a bipap machine on my face to help me breathe. They wheeled me in, and I sat in my chair nervously. There were four people: one with the spray to numb my throat, one assisting nurse, one holding the bipap to my face, and one anaesthesiologist.

As they removed the bipap and sprayed my throat to numb it, I coughed repeatedly, feeling the liquid slip into my lungs. I panted hard, like a dog in heat. My heart raced, and I felt dazed. They sprayed again, and the same thing happened.

I was worn out, and they were running out of time. They inserted the tube down my unfrozen throat, and the whole time I felt pain as it rubbed against my vocal chords. She couldn't get it in. I moaned and made noises for her to remove it. She pulled it out, and they quickly put the bipap back on my face. I gasped and could barely catch a breath. I felt my respiratory system shutting down.

I looked at the nurse. "Why are you crying?" I mouthed.

She rubbed my head and said, "It's just sad, honey."

They attempted the procedure again. She inserted the tube, this time fishing around for much longer. I wasn't breathing. Not a single breath. I moaned and gagged as the plastic rubbed down into my chest. Nothing. I squeezed the nurses hand with a surge of power. I stared deep into her eyes and thought, "This is it. I'm going to die."

"33% oxygen!" I heard her yell as she removed the tube, and I began to black out. She pulled it out, which didn't make a lot of difference because I still couldn't breathe. I felt my bowels and bladder empty completely. They put me onto a stretcher. I was not getting a single breath of air. They put me to sleep, and then I was out.

Over the next week, the doctors told my parents that there was a 75% chance I was going to die and that they should tell everyone to come say their goodbyes. So they all came, leaving cards and stuffed animals. For the first few days, my pneumonia worsened until they found the right antibiotic.

After nine days, I awoke to find my mom sitting at my bed. Unable to talk, I looked around. My mom smiled and started talking to me, explaining what had happened. My dad and sister came up to see me later. They told me that everyone had come to see me and that everyone had prayed for me.

While I was sleeping, they increased my Prednisone dosage to 60mg daily and gave me five plasmapheresis treatments. During the next three days they kept me on the respirator, just in case I still needed it. It was the most uncomfortable thing I'd ever experienced, and I kept writing to the doctor to take it out. After I'd spent eleven days in the ICU, they removed the tube, and, after one more night to ensure my improvement, they moved me to a ward.

My sister came to see me every single day after work, and I could tell just by looking in her eyes that she was scared to death of losing me. Kristy and Holly came up to see me, and I was perked up and waiting with energy. Three peas in a pot, the nickname we used to describe our close friendship, was written all over the cards and pictures they had made for me.

"You did G-raffe on your death bed," they exclaimed.

One time, while we were all high, we had, for some odd reason, said "G-raffe" and, at the same time, turned our heads to the side, extending our necks like giraffes. After that, whenever we'd see each other, we'd yell, "G-raffe!" and do the movement.

"What do you mean, I did G-raffe on my death bed?"

"What do you mean, what do I mean? You did G-raffe on you're death bed. You couldn't talk or open your eyes, but I whispered G-raffe in your ear, and you did it."

I was shocked and found great amusement in this. They left that night, and I was in great spirits. I was doing better, and, after another week in the neurology ICU, they sent me home. I still couldn't shake the guilty feeling that all this had happened because of me. I had smoked so much pot that I gave myself pneumonia.

CHAPTER 13 –
CHANGES FOR A FUTURE

I returned home to my beautiful room, the room I had spent so much time on and in. I rolled up to the door, which had remained closed the entire duration of my hospital stay. No one was allowed in. I examined my door, which was covered with pictures and paintings that my gang and I had drawn while in "artistic mode."

I turned the door knob, which had a cheetah hanging around it with the words "You! Stay out of my jungle!" on it. I pushed the door open and glared at my animal covered bed, which fit the jungle theme. My walls and furniture were baby blue, my favorite color. The walls were covered with posters of my favorite rappers, a Mariah Carey shrine, a wall of get well cards, and collages that Kristy and I had made while bored. My mirror was 65% covered with stickers, photo booth pictures, and decorations with my name on them. In one corner hung a rainbow-colored net filled with an endless amount of stuffed animals that had been given to me throughout the years. Multicolored butterflies dangled from the ceiling by yellow shiny fishing line. The dresser was completely covered with lotions, perfumes, make-up, candles, and other little goodies. There was a little section for my stuffed giraffes, my favorite animal. Dangling from the ceiling was my beautiful, vast collection of fifteen wind chimes which complimented the assortment of figurines on the shelf across from them. My entertainment center was filled with all my interests, crochet yarn, my chess set, my painting and arts and craft supplies, and my karaoke machine and CDs.

I smiled as I tapped on my glass fish tank. "Hello, lil' guys," I said to my fishes.

My room was like a giant art project and reflected my personality perfectly. I loved the way my room made me feel, and it was good to be home again.

* * *

I was doing better at home taking 60mg of Prednisone daily. I was still on Cellcept and Mestinon as well. I continued to have plasmapheresis on a weekly basis. I went to see my neurologist, and we decided to cut the Prednisone back from 60mg to 50mg and, eventually, to none at all. I would continue the Cytoxan monthly and go to plasmapheresis every other week.

I started to reduce the Prednisone, and, by the time I got to 50mg alternating with 25mg, my breathing was affected. I was much weaker, and I had to go back to the all-too-familiar emergency room. This time, we avoided intubation. They kept me on the bipap, increased my Prednisone to 60mg again, and sent me home feeling better.

In December, we increased the Prednisone dosage to alternate between 150mg one day and 25mg the next, which gave me a boost along with some extra pounds. I began exercising, taking short walks, and pedaling the bicycle for hours a day. I continued getting plasmapheresis every other week. We reduced the Mestinon dosage and increased the Cellcept and Cytoxan dosages.

In October, I began to get low fevers and pain in my line. I went into the hospital to have a new line inserted when we discovered that it was infected. I hadn't eaten for about ten days, and my potassium levels were extremely low, which was also causing weakness. They gave me some antibiotics and potassium, and, after two weeks, my infection was gone, and I had yet again avoided another ICU situation.

* * *

Christmas came, and I had spent all of my savings on my family, getting them whatever they wanted and then some. I wanted to make up for all the hurt that our family had been through by buying them the things they wanted. If I couldn't be better, I could at least bring some joy to them this way. On Christmas Eve, we had Kristy's family and a bunch of friends over. We all got drunk, opened presents, and ate Christmas dinner. It was a great Christmas, and everyone enjoyed spending time together.

Holly, Kristy and me on Christmas Eve.

* * *

I continued to have Cytoxan each month, increasing the dosage after the doctor saw my blood work go to the proper levels. We reduced the Prednisone again, this time alternating between 125mg and 25mg, and increased the Cellcept to 3 grams a day. I continued to exercise, which also increased my appetite. I continued to eat a lot over the months because of the Prednisone. I now weighed 350 pounds. I was trying hard to keep my eating down, and I lost 12 lbs.

Then I heard the devastating news. My sweet mom was now terminally ill with cancer. It was in her lungs and had spread to her lymph nodes. I regained the weight I had worked hard to lose and was now completely frustrated. The stress from worrying about my mom was making my myasthenia worse, and I had put my school work on hold because I wasn't able to focus, a side affect of the Prednisone and stress I was under.

* * *

Although the road ahead sometimes looks dull for me, I always look to my family and friends, and they give me the strength to carry on with life. I have a wonderful neurologist who has tried every possible avenue to save me.

My health still isn't where I'd like it to be, and it may never get to that point, but all I can do is try my hardest to achieve the goals and dreams I have set for myself as well as be a role model for my younger brother and other people out there who struggle with illness. I have started seeing a dietitian and have since lost 15 pounds, which is a start.

I took the frustration, depression, happiness, and all the other emotions I felt and put them towards something positive, writing my book. It's been a long and hard struggle, and I know I have a way to go. I will continue on this journey that has been set before me and help my mom until the end as she once helped me.

Life is a choice of choices, and, in order to make it better, you must make the right choices and hope for the best. If you make the wrong choices, don't dwell on it, because it's never too late to make things right again.

I have come so far with the love and support from the people around me. There's no way I could ever give up, because that would mean that all the extra love and care that my family, friends and doctors have put into me was for nothing. I continue to take things one day at a time, and I realize that, no matter how bad things get, there's always a pot of gold at the end of the rainbow.

Like a giraffe, my adaptation to my surroundings and to life has made it possible for me to survive, and I will forever be that little giraffe girl.

POEMS

THE MAIL

It's so strange,
How time flies by,
All these memories,
Fresh in my mind.
I try to think about yesterday,
When I was happy,
But my most horrid memories,
Come back and slap me.
I try to forget,
But I just can't.
The things you did,
The words you rant.
This is now,
That was then,
You're my lucky star,
And my best friend.
I know you don't believe me,
And the trust is gone,
But I just want you to know,
I forgive you mom.

MOM

As my head lies on the window sill,
The warm spring beats down on me.
I close my eyes,
And drift off to the sound of birds and bees swishing through the air.
I then start thinking of my troubles,
And how I can stop them.
My mind is cluttered with traffic.
All my worries rewind and replay again,
I start to cry.
Tears stream down my face,
And my emotions run wild.
The sweet essence of spring overpowers me.
The hot sun dries my tears,
And I breathe deep.
All my tensions are released.
A butterfly floats over to me,
She tells me it'll be okay.
I believe her words,
And I smile.

LOST FOREVER

Suffocating
Like being stuck in a safe.
No one knows you're there,
Crying out
Legs heavy
Like eyes drooping,
I fall
So unhappy,
Unfair,
Why me?
A tiger deprived of his stripes,
childhood stolen,
What I knew, loved—lost forever
Yet I must go on
Determined, strong minded.

BE GREAT TOMORROW

tainted
fainted; together braided
a pretty picture is painted
so mistaken
thoughts shaken
I am agitated
secretly screaming
smile misleading
eyes deceiving
mind leaving
yet drawn back slowly
like a fishing hook
searching for glory
overpower the sorrow
ill survive today
be great tomorrow

LAY ON MY PILLOW

Lay on my pillow
feel the tears
harbor the pain
overshadowed by fears

See through my eyes
watch the days go by
nothing to do
but sit and cry

UNTITLED

Energy in my soul
trying to escape
but physically distorted
why can't I be me?
Exciting, happy
overwhelmed by weakness
and insecurities.

ESCAPE

One day,
One hour,
One minute.
A full breath sigh of relief,
An uncrooked smile,
A sparkling eye, wide open.
A strong stand,
A dream fulfilled,
For
One day,
One hour,
One minute,
Of escape.

THE MOST BEAUTIFUL GIRL

My smile isn't the whitest
My hair isn't the finest
I don't have the smoothest skin
I'm not the smallest
My eyes aren't the bluest
But I'm the most beautiful girl
you'll ever meet.

UNTITLED

That long-lost breath,
I never saw it comin'
If only I had stopped pretending
to be
Superwoman.

THE BRISK

trees are bare
not a leaf can be found
nothing to bloom
just freezing ice-covered ground

the days are dark and dead
the air is crisp
my mind is wandering
out in the brisk

FIREPLACE

I'm so cold
I can't think
I'm half awake
drifting in and out
of reality

infatuation with fire
keeps me warm
and conscious
coming back,
again and again.

This is my reflection time.

ALLIGATORS

Carefully crossing a suspension bridge
with a puddle underneath
avoiding the alligators.

Alligators come after me
Jumping, bouncing
off the water
I escape them.

I sit on the balcony
overlooking the water
with the alligators surrounding,
antagonizing me.

RODGER

It's been a while since I saw you last,
And I especially miss your voice.
All your smiles and sweet things you did,
To leave was not your choice.

A son,
A dad,
A brother,
An uncle
And above all a wonderful friend,
such a caring and courageous person,
and his life came to an end.

Through all the times of tears and sorrow,
And our family was corrupt,
You put us back together again,
And lifted our spirits up.

And even when we were mad at you,
And our relationship got off track,
Your charisma and soft blue eyes,
Always won us back.

And when that day comes around each year,
From us you had to part,
I look at your picture and smile and cry,
And your face overwhelms my heart.

Now you're gone and we're without you,
And I miss you like the rest,
But after all this time I've figured out,
God only takes the best.

FOR KRISTY

Thank you friend,
For just being you.
For putting up with me,
when I wasn't true.

Thank you friend,
For making me laugh,
For not letting me cry,
For keeping me tough.

Thank you friend,
For holding your ground,
For speaking your mind,
For making me proud.

Thank you my friend,
For bringing me cheer,
For lending a hand,
For just being there.

Thank you Kristy,
for on you I depend,
If you ever need me,
I'll be there.
That's why we're best friends.

BUD

Brother have I told you lately how important you are to me?
How I cherish you so much?
How my heart, you have touched?

You have made me into a better person, kind, happy and determined.

Brother have I told you lately how you're always on my mind?
How I think of you day and night?
How I hope that you're all right?
Don't worry, all smiles, no fury.

Brother have I told you lately I miss you?
How I miss your sweet ways?
How I miss how we would play?
The way you blink those almond eyes, the way you laugh,
      the way you cry.

Brother have I told you lately how proud I am of you?
Of how good your marks are?
Of how you throw the ball so far?
How well you cope, your achievements, how high you climb the rope.

Brother have I told you lately how much I appreciate you?
You made me see, gave me love and support and so much you've
     taught me.

Brother have I told you lately how special you are?
How there's only one Bud, not two.
How I wish I was you?
You're so perfect, caring and true.
I love you.

LOSING MOM

I cry every day
because
I'm going to lose you.

I can only hope I have
given to you
as much as you
have given to me.

I'm so sorry it has
to be this way
and that you
won't be here to
experience this beautiful life
you have given us.

I know you're scared
and you're not ready to
leave us.

If only there was another way.
A choice. But there isn't.

And all I can do is cry.
Cry for the grandkids you'll
never get to hold, my husband you'll
never get to meet and the miracle,
you'll never get to witness.

I love you so much and no
matter how hard I cry, it doesn't
change the fact that I'm losing the
person who gave me life, the
person who sat by my bed in ICU, the
person who held me dear as I cried,
my best friend, my sweet mom.

I can only hope and pray you
don't suffer and that you go
peacefully in your sleep.
You've suffered enough
and you don't deserve this.

Be brave Mom and fight until
the end, like you taught me.
Then go into the night and
shine down on us, our little angel,
in heaven.

3 1221 08255 4671

Printed in the United States
64418LVS00002B/1-3